Contents;

Tree Murmurs.

This booklet seeks to explore the inner language of trees and their murmurs of past wisdom.

There is within Britain an exceptional tradition known to Druids in past ages. It is still alive for those who choose to listen and observe the trees in their seasons.

Trees, once widely revered, lent great wisdom to men's lives. We communed between our selves and the trees, and were deeply at one with the universe.

Some trees were of enormous importance. They represented aspects of our developing inner lives. An eternal tree cycle, reflecting the dynamics of the universal soul unfolding, integrates this inner circle of native trees.

This ancient British wisdom is difficult to access. It is hoped that these simple poems, echoing the various qualities of these trees and bushes, will reveal some of the sensitivity toward nature that once prevailed in our beautiful isles.

The trees were great companions to those who chose to study or contemplate life's mysteries. Today we can still explore that relationship and sometimes, when we stand in quiet shadows, sun dappled dell, or windswept moors, we can even imagine how it was.

Our journey starts at midwinter, when the elm and birch celebrate new life, or life after death. A diagram, shown on the centre pages, illustrates this. The sequence of trees portrays the seasons coming full circle. The geometric pattern formed depicts the soul's striving for perfection or God realisation.

Five **vowel trees** sit within the centre of the diagram and are interspersed at regular intervals throughout the **consonant trees** which are shown on the outer ring. Each vowel represents a short season, and each consonant a lunar month.

E.g. Elm represents the vowel **A** (for Ailm), and belongs to late winter. Three consonant trees share this time of year with this key vowel tree. They are first of all the birch, followed by the rowan, and lastly the ash. Their Gaelic translations are given, and we can see that in Gaelic, the name of each of these trees began with a consonant.

It is believed that the consonant trees signified more distinct soul qualities inherent in the individual trees, while the vowel trees stood for a prevailing soul mood that enveloped the short season or cluster of specific trees.

The diagram also shows the various Celtic festivals. A brief description of these is given on page 20.

With most of the trees is a short description of its astrological attributes, its prominence in the Celtic year, and its qualities.

This information is displayed in the format;

RULING PLANET / ELEMENT / SEASON / Qualities.

Any comments regarding accuracy of the material contained in this booklet should be directed to Jackie Queally of Celtic Trails Scotland. Historical literature and archaeological evidence is often open to interpretation and Jackie will be very happy to discuss the sources of the material she has used if it varies from your own understanding.

ELM (A - Ailm)

I prolong
the dense quietness
that binds us to this earth.

I follow on with destiny,
the wheel that leads to rebirth,
the Tree of Life.

I thrive in open spaces
or shady streams.
A flourishing of limbs
sensing space, ascending
in glorious sweeps, descending
in benign stoops, bowing
to foragers' delight.

A simple grace
now rarer,
that scoops the air.
I, descendent of Eden
reserve
my place.

***

SATURN / EARTH / SUMMER, AUTUMN /
Purification. Love. Light. Wisdom.

Elms Twig

Young Elms

BIRCH

I grace the skies
with slender forms
embracing space
like none other.
And Venus beckons me
to her chamber
to rest my weary limbs
against the greying skies.
She bathes me with all her love
and restores me.
I will give you life
wherever you are
whether you are
alone or in company
near or far.
Why hesitate?
I seek your bidding
at the beginning
of the year.

***

VENUS / AIR & WATER / SPRING & AUTUMN / Healing.
New beginnings. Mysteries of young goddess.

ROWAN

I am the fire of effervescence
solar - led
beads of fire perspiring
in a fountain of release.

Light - illuminating spirals deflecting
loss of wholeness.

Protected, I lead you
to your world of higher senses
preparing your descent again.
Within, without, you turn,
you mirror me, and grow.
Return, blessed and whole.

***

SUN / FIRE / SPRING & AUTUMN / Protects ley lines and stone circles. Protects against enchantment. healing. Highest pure magic. Control of all senses. Psychic powers. Success.

Rowan

ASH

I eagle - eye the forest,
swoop and scoop the unrevealed
whilst soaring upward to the sun.
Beneath me my Mother the Earth
feeding me deep waters from her womb.

I am a spear thrust upwards
sap rising towards my Father the Sun

My cry delves deep into brown veins:
"I am the spirit of survival!
The spirit of Success.
The flowing milk of the season!"

***

SUN / WATER / SUMMER / Inner and outer worlds linked.
Polarities. Quick intellect.

Young Ash

Ash leaf

ALDER

I come from the ancient lands
when water was abundant
and Knowledge too.

If my shape is shrouded in mystery,
my shield can still protect you -
unknown depths lurk.

Believe in my blessedness.
Respect my threshold.
Receive my smouldering fire.

I am the invisible spark
of inner will,
honouring the darkness still
in the need to fulfil
my destiny.
Some see a noble sacrifice
of strength -
but these deepest, darkest parts
cast in patient vigil
bear a flame invisible.

I seek you
in your hour
of greatest transformation -
I await you still.

***

Alder

VENUS / WATER / SPRING & SUMMER / Divination.
Oracular Heads. Protects self & country.

GORSE (O - Onn)

I occupy the eternal soils of youth
whose lessons are cloaked in adversity
and fruits are bruised with sweetness
for the bees.
Delicate blooms of yellow brightness
enveloped by the goddess'
coconut - sweet breathing
eternal in her love.

Ah! I am vigour!
ferocious fire,
stubborn fire,
borne of stubborn wood stems
star - leaved in their nakedness.
Live on…

***

Star-leaves

Bloom

WILLOW

I carry the gentle mystery of hope
in the spaces I weave.
Leaning like tentacles
eagerly clutching
visions of the night
brought back
into the Light.
I hover on the edge of the Dreamtime
enveloping the Well of water Divine.
No time for Death,
nor yet for Life alone.
A sense of something else -
A surgeon carving stitches on your soul
so your fears drop off
one by one.
The journey completed
once embarked upon,
yet renewed
moment by moment.
I dissipate pain.

***

MOON / WATER / SPRING & SAMHAIN / Dowsing. Psychism via water. Night visions. Lunar tides & magic. Ability to forgive and forget. Non-piteous, correct view of self.

Willow

Willow

BLACKTHORN

I conjure up my purgative fumes,
and then
I stoke the flames,
inverting flames
of inner molten states
into a stubborn fire.

Wielding the Old Hag
upon the Innocent
and yielding fruits
of the unfathomable.

***

(fruit)MARS, (plant)SATURN / FIRE / IMBOLC & LATE AUTUMN /
Cleansing Karmic issues. Lack of choice but still hopeful.

Sloes (Blackthorn berries)

HAWTHORN

Hawthorn berries

I am the feminine,
with fire so strong
that I remain;
untouched,
unadulterated,
at one with the Divas -
but not with men
who long for me.

My celibacy celebrated in sun-kissed berries.
Honour me, and I will protect you.

My affinities are almost boundless.

I am of the alluring wild -
and not of gardenkind.

***

MARS / FIRE / BELTANE & AUTUMN / Fertility. Guardian.
Cleansing. Door to other world. Happiness.

Hawthorn blossom

OAK

I am the sun warrior triumphant
standing guard to the aeons,
protecting
Earth with my eternal oath.
In between the threshold
lies the crack
there am I -
the sun warrior triumphant
standing steadfast at the door.
I, protector of the Earth
gathering forces in untouched realms
undeterred by the creatures of linear time,
in a constant state of expectancy.
The initiated recognise
my presence.
My seed
waits patiently,
forever ripening,
solemnly toasting
the future kingdom.

***

SATURN / EARTH / SUMMER & AUTUMN / Purification. Love.
Light. Elves. Wisdom. Carries on regardless of troubles.
Courage and strength.

Oak dell   Oak leaves

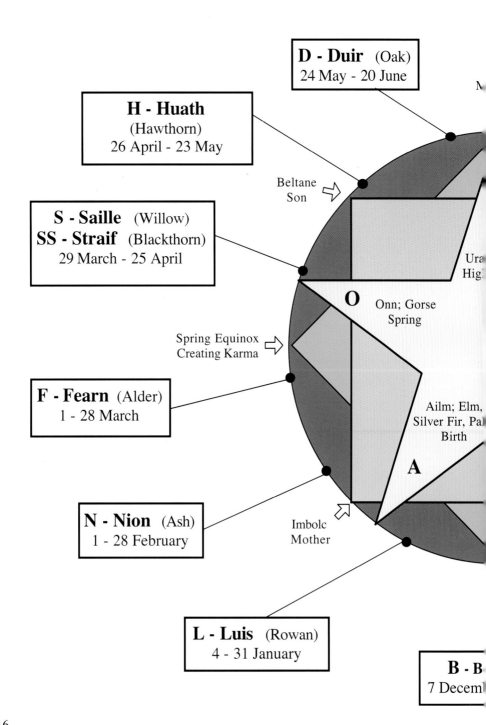

D - Duir (Oak)
24 May - 20 June

H - Huath
(Hawthorn)
26 April - 23 May

S - Saille (Willow)
SS - Straif (Blackthorn)
29 March - 25 April

Beltane
Son

Ura
Hig

O Onn; Gorse
Spring

Spring Equinox
Creating Karma

F - Fearn (Alder)
1 - 28 March

Ailm; Elm,
Silver Fir, Pa
Birth

A

N - Nion (Ash)
1 - 28 February

Imbolc
Mother

L - Luis (Rowan)
4 - 31 January

B - B
7 Decem

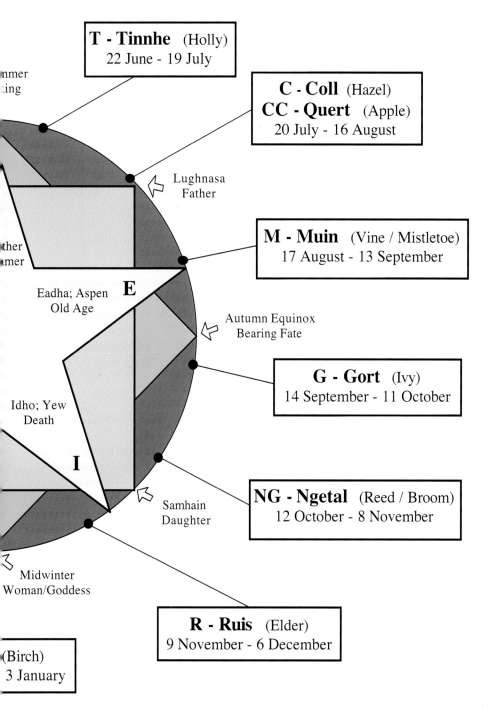

T - Tinnhe (Holly)
22 June - 19 July

C - Coll (Hazel)
CC - Quert (Apple)
20 July - 16 August

nmer
:ing

Lughnasa
Father

ther
:mer

M - Muin (Vine / Mistletoe)
17 August - 13 September

Eadha; Aspen
Old Age

E

Autumn Equinox
Bearing Fate

G - Gort (Ivy)
14 September - 11 October

Idho; Yew
Death

I

NG - Ngetal (Reed / Broom)
12 October - 8 November

Samhain
Daughter

Midwinter
Woman/Goddess

R - Ruis (Elder)
9 November - 6 December

(Birch)
3 January

17

The Celtic Year.

In considering the thirteen months of the year and their respective tree spirits, it is helpful to study the eight festivals within the normal year.

In divine terms, there is a transfer of power at **midsummer** from the old god to the new one at this time of year. In human terms, the **boy becomes man**. The holly king succeeds the oak king at this point, but with one other significant item to bear in mind: there was an extra day set aside each year, which belonged to none of the lunar months.

In the gap between the kings, in midsummer, the endless cycle of generations was suspended. In Celtic mythology life after death is set in a summer paradise. This seems rather akin to the way in which the pause between the out-breath and the in-breath in yogic breathing is deemed significant for spiritual insight. A glimpse of eternity may well enter the pause between the breaths of separate years. At this point, heroes mingle with the deities, and anything is possible. We still have the expression "midsummer madness".

The high summer seems to align itself with the element of light or fire. The New Year begun, the **old king** is still commemorated at **Lughnasa** from mid July until mid August. In the Welsh Mabinogion, Lugh lives in Avallon – the eternal apple orchard – feasting on apples and hazelnuts which come to fruit during Lughnasa.

The **Autumn Equinox** would not have been fixed at 21st September, as it depended on the intervals of the full moon, but it was in late September, and was probably a minor festival associated with Bran who was the father of the Underworld. This is during the month of the Ivy, and is concerned with life after death. Bran's influence is rather ambiguous. Set midway between the old father and the **virgin daughter**, it would suggest the dark hand of fate.

At **Samhain** in early November, the archetypal **daughter** is prominent – she is the Virgin Princess. Courage and pain is involved, but like Rhiannon in the Mabinogian; the power is with the goddess in this season, and there are close associations with the yew.

At **midwinter** the mystery of this girl is incarnated as the **girl becomes woman** and potential mother through the gift of **fertility**. This is the time of Brigit, when the Birch tree of inception holds sway. It is also a time of great healing. The first half has a quality of inwardly preparing the psyche for the second half, which is more to do with action in the physical world. The first half can also be seen as a time for reflection on one's actions.

Motherhood itself comes to the fore at **Imbolc** in the second half of the year. Brigit continues her influence here as protectress of women in labour and childbirth. The festival of the first ewe's milk was around the beginning of February. After winter, the milk was starting to flow again, and this could be taken as another sign that the mysteries of motherhood were prominent.

The **Spring Equinox**, like its counterpart in the darker side of the year, is connected with Bran of the Alder tree. Here the opposite of Autumn's fatalistic viewpoint comes into play – there is instead an emphasis on the hero who by correct speech and noble deeds brings about change. It is the time when fate can be challenged successfully, and **new karma** struck.

At **Beltane** in early May the Sun god Bel is celebrated. At this point in the year, the **son** is also highlighted. As the son grows older, his power grows also, and he needs to practise vigilance. It requires all the inward strength the son can muster. Behind the outward show of power, the mystery of the goddess who bore him in the darkest part of the year is waiting to be incarnated. Beltane offers him a real chance for growth, provided he is wise enough. If he should succeed, the endless karmic cycle can end…. Of course, the usual pattern is for the son to merely topple the father at midsummer and for the cycle to begin again! The chaste hawthorn here epitomises the psychic power needed to meet the challenges set.

The element of fire and the witchcraft of Bran combine here. The Druids saw the need for purifying themselves at this time of year.

There are four main elements in the physical world, and the cycle of the year encompasses these neatly. They are as follows:

Air	first quarter.
Water	second quarter, culminating in midwinter.
Earth	third quarter.
Fire	fourth quarter, culminating at midsummer.

Finally, there are five "tree-vowels" which fit in with the pattern of the year. In the times of the Druids, the vowels were linked within the calendar like a five-pointed star. When placed within the eightfold path of festivals and the thirteen-fold sequence of months, it can be seen how beautifully these soul-alignments fitted into the scheme.

HEATHER (U - Ura)

Dream on
diviner of secrets.
I am the flow for
your optimistic surrender.
I guide your juices
until
love manifests
in all its myriad forms.

***

Fading Heather

HOLLY

I am the king who heralds in
all that is good and wholesome,
and indeed holy.
My iron splendid
adorns the space
I viscous ly defend.

I grow old and tough
the very stuff
of the most victorious.
Pass me by, and hearken to
my blessing

Use it for universal good.

***

MARS / FIRE / MIDWINTER / Strongest protective herb. Clear wisdom
& courage. Dream magic. Generous hearted trusting.

Holly

21

HAZEL

I wave my wand with fairer face,
mine is a noble grace.
I impart Wisdom
and cast light on the shadows
with my enduring powers.
I long to show
my treasures.
But only those who approach
with due care
can commune
with my treasures bound beyond
the shimmering sheen
of diamond pinnacles
sky - bound;
beyond the silver waters
of deepest wells earthbound.
I satisfy and end your search,
your thirst, your hunger
and potentize your memory.

***

(nuts) MERCURY, (plant) SUN / AIR / IMBOLC & AUTUMN /
Intuition. Divining. Dowsing. Individuality. Power to find the hidden.

Hazel

Hazelnuts

CRABAPPLE

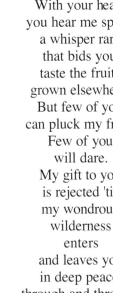

I dwell within the inner core
weaving the dreams
that sees and feels the seasons
form an endless world.
With your heart
you hear me speak
a whisper rare
that bids you
taste the fruits
grown elsewhere.
But few of you
can pluck my fruit.
Few of you
will dare.
My gift to you
is rejected 'til
my wondrous
wilderness
enters
and leaves you
in deep peace,
through and through.

***

VENUS / WATER / ALL SEASONS / Healing love. Poetic inspiration.
Works of destiny. Self-love and self-acceptance.

Crabapple in blossom

BLACKBERRY

Sweet am I,
an enigma of sorts;
I blend in,
I bend around,
I bow low,
and ramble on.

My humble fruit
gives sustenance.

Come - eat of me.

***

SUN / AIR / MIDSUMMER & WINTER SOLSTICE /
Visitation of divine. The hidden. Wands. Fertility of gods.

Blackberry fruit

ASPEN (E - Eadha)

I travel on the wings of time and space,
seeking out the spirit spots that listen
with a keening ear.
Their music echoed in my trembling
delicate vibrations wavering
all tuned to worlds we cannot see
and have all but forgotten
in our quest for
popularity.

The lone poplar
growing old in good company and grace
is I, is I, is I.

I court death wisely
measuring man's time and space,
benign bestower.
But who listens now?

***

MERCURY / AIR / AUTUMN & WINTER / Eloquence. Psychic Gifts
from the wind. Aid to rebirth. Prevention of illness.

Aspen

Aspen Leaf

IVY

I offer you only frenzied glimpses
of what lies between
one world and another.

Spiralling a web of dreams
the green goddess knows
which are her own.

My one eternal breath
feeds your yearning
and spins the turning
resurrecting of your soul.

***

Ivy

BROOM

I, the battered monarch,
the wind whistling through
and shaken to the fibres.
Intact I remain
to reassure you,
with later fragrant
blooms of promise.

***

Broom

Broom in Bloom

Reed

REED

Royal veins,
fed by silt,
set me apart
as noble,
and upright.

***

Reed

YEW (I - Iubhar)

I am as deep as darkness
I bestow beauty on shadow -
illuminating depths,
and in my silence
I echo a primitive eternity.
I serve the seasons in my stillness.
I guard the secrets to the world beyond
come through my gate
and behold,
beyond.

***

SATURN / EARTH / WINTER / Guardian to threshold of rebirth.
Rest after struggle of life. Divination. Bows.

Yew

ELDER

I oversee the cauldron
surrounded by my good folk
who love,
and court, the night.
I withstand decay wrought upon
my long suffering earth.
I await my transformation
from old hag into maiden
yet again.
Death cannot be delayed.
Embrace it tenderly,
for I remain
to guard your spirit,
wrapping you sweetly
in my warm embrace.

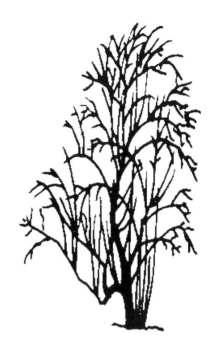

***

VENUS / EARTH / EARLY SUMMER & LATE AUTUMN /
Regeneration. Cauldron of rebirth.

Elder berries

Elder flowers